51 Must Know Facts About Human Body

BESTSELLING NON-FICTION

- Abraham Lincoln by Lord Charnwood, ISBN: 9789380914251
- Annihilation of Caste by Dr B.R. Ambedkar, ISBN: 9789390492732
- Be What You Wish by Neville Goddard, ISBN: 9789387669550
- Civilization and Its Discontents by Sigmund Freud, ISBN: 9789387669499
- Guerrilla Warfare by Ernesto Che Guevara, ISBN: 9789354990366
- How I Made 2 Millions in the Stock Market by N. Darvas, ISBN: 9789389716283
- Jail Diary and Other Writings by Bhagat Singh, ISBN: 9789390492398
- Man-eaters of Kumaon by Jim Corbett, ISBN: 9789354990731
- My Experiments with Truth by Mahatma Gandhi, ISBN: 9789387669291
- Relativity by Albert Einstein, ISBN: 9789380914220
- Reminiscences of a Stock Operator by Edwin Lefevre, ISBN: 9788194764816
- Scientific Healing Affirmations by P. Yogananda, ISBN: 9789389716344
- Student's Encyclopedia of G.K. by Azeem Ahmad Khan, ISBN: 9789380914190
- The Art of War by Sun Tzu, ISBN: 9789380914893
- The Book of Five Rings by Miyamoto Musashi, ISBN: 9789354991202
- The Diary of a Young Girl by Anne Frank, ISBN: 9789380914312
- The Game of Life and How to Play It by F. Scovel Shinn, ISBN: 9789387669390
- The Law of Success by Napoleon Hill, ISBN: 9788180320927
- The Origin of Species by Charles Darwin, ISBN: 9788180320453
- The Power of Your Subconscious Mind by Joseph Murphy, ISBN: 9788180320958
- The Psychopathology of Everyday Life by Sigmund Freud, ISBN: 9789388118071
- The Richest Man in Babylon by George S. Clason, ISBN: 9789387669369
- The World as I See It by Albert Einstein, ISBN: 9789388118125
- Why I am an Atheist and Other Works by Bhagat Singh, ISBN: 9789354992162
- Zen in the Art of Archery by Eugen Herrigel, ISBN: 9789354991059

Search the book by its ISBN

51 MUST KNOW FACTS ABOUT

HUMAN BODY

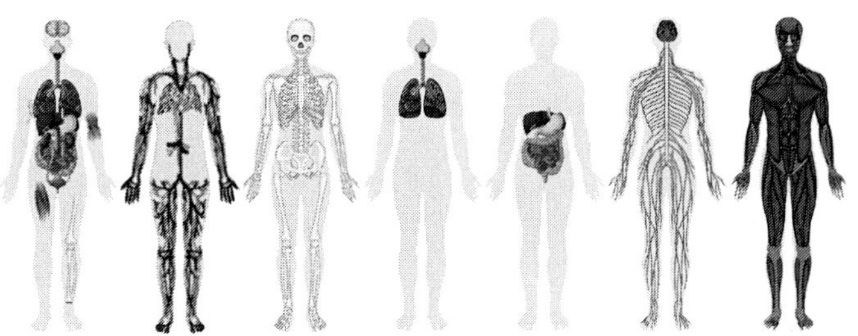

GENERAL PRESS

Published by
GENERAL PRESS

4805/24, Fourth Floor, Krishna House
Ansari Road, Daryaganj, New Delhi - 110002
Ph : 011-23282971, 45795759
E-mail : generalpressindia@gmail.com

www.generalpress.in

First Edition : 2023

ISBN : 9789354996467

Published by Azeem Ahmad Khan for General Press

Contents

Introduction

The human body is an incredible living, breathing, moving, eating, thinking and interactive machine. Your body is an unimaginable gift, inside which there are millions of profound parts working together amazingly to keep you alive in a healthy and active way. Each body is an individual with its own unique personality differences, yet is constructed and works in a very similar manner. There are still some wondrous mysteries that have not yet been figured out.

The human body is pretty smart when you think about all the things it does. Human beings are unlike most other creatures—walk upright on two legs and create ideas using brains and hands. The body grows bigger, builds new body parts to replace old ones, repairs itself if it gets injured, has special parts to sense light, sounds, smells, tastes and objects.

Learn and explore the most fascinating facts about your body with '51 Must Know Facts about Human Body'. Discover the sensational systems and senses, magnificent structures, all revealed in an exciting, simplified and intriguing approach. You will be impelled to care for your wonderful body, once you find out the amazing things it does for you!

51

MUST KNOW FACTS ABOUT HUMAN BODY

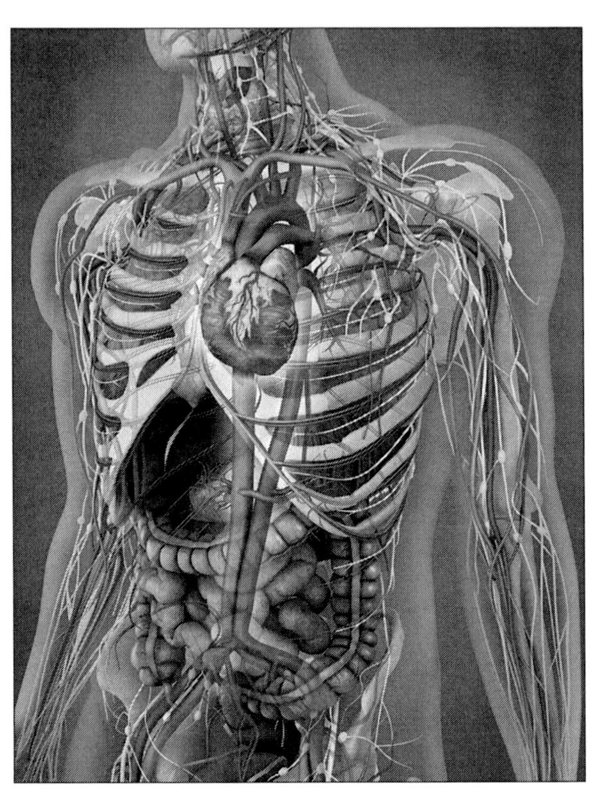

FACT NUMBER

1

Humans have a remarkable ability to adapt to a variety of lifestyles in contrasting locations. We may appear different from the outside, with our own individualities, but under the skin, our bodies look the same and work in identical ways.

2

Human body is the most complex of all organisms, able to perform an extraordinary range of functions, and is made up of more than 100,000 billion microscopic living units called cells, each with its own unique complexities, and each of which can divide up to 50 times before dying. Similar cells join together (mitosis) to form a tissue, two or more tissues make an organ, which are linked together to create twelve body systems. An estimated 50,000 cells are replaced every second in the human body by means of cellular division.

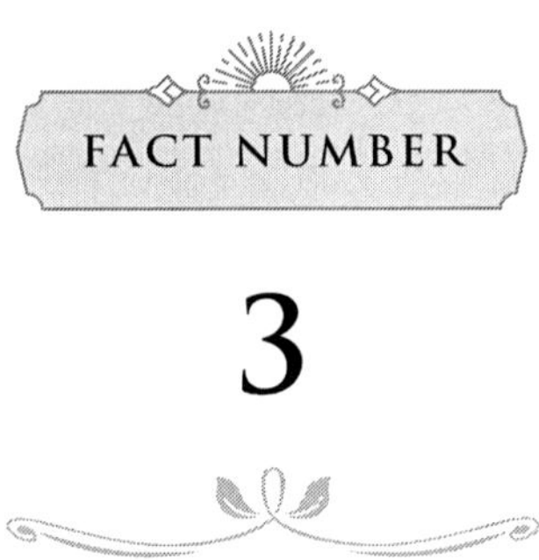

3

The study of anatomy explores body structures, showing that internally all bodies are constructed in the similar way—except for differences between males and females. Artists of Renaissance, such as Leonardo da Vinci (1452-1519), were among the first to make precise drawings of bones for the study of anatomy. The skeletal system is a strong structure made up of 206 bones and their supporting ligaments and cartilage. It gives the body form, protects the internal organs and makes movement possible.

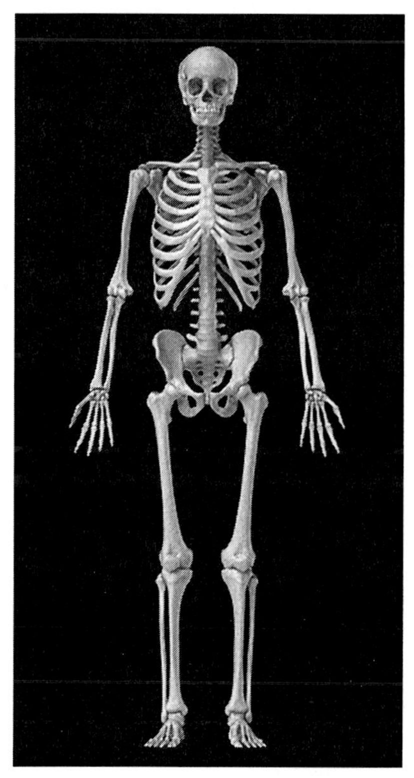

Human Body 15

4

The bones store minerals and produce blood cells in the bone marrow. The total number of bones in the adult body is usually 206 and the number of teeth is 32. A small bone is capable of supporting up to 9 tons without breaking. 3 mm is the length of the shortest bone in the body—the Stirrup, a bone in the ear. The thigh bone called the Femur, is the largest bone in the human body—48 cm in length. The most flexible joint in the entire human body is the shoulder joint. Over a person's lifetime the bones are continuously regenerated—this process continues even after reaching maturity. The weight of an average human head is 4 kg, representing about 7% of the total body weight. Hands and feet contain more than half of the bones in the entire body.

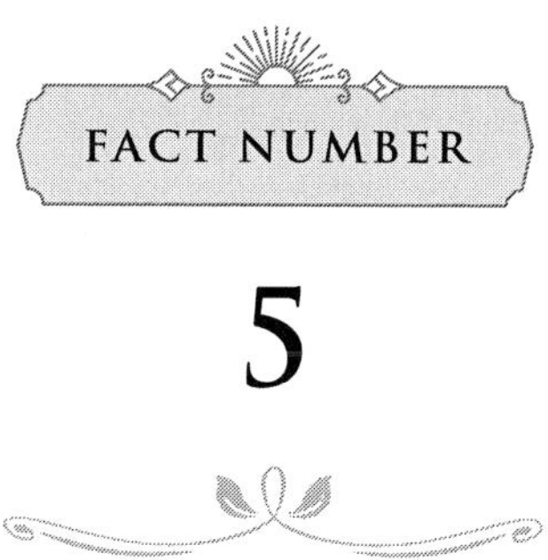

5

Consists of a series of bones chained together (vertebrae)—the spinal column lends support to the body and forms a protective inner channel through which the spinal cord runs. The ribs shield the vital internal organs, which include the heart and lungs. The sounds made by joints, such as the cracking of knuckles are caused by an explosive release of gas that permits shock-absorbing fluid to flow in. The only bone in the human body that does not form a joint with any other bone is the bone in the throat called the hyoid bone. It helps keep the trachea open and forms a connection with your tongue muscles. Bones are also natural healers. Calcium keeps the bones strong and healthy. The pelvis is the biggest bone in the body, made up of 6 bones held closely together. The male pelvis is smaller and narrower than the female pelvis.

6

Making up 40% of the body weight—the muscles are organs that shape and protect the body. They are formed by millions of muscle fibers, neatly arranged in rows. They are divided into striated, smooth and in a unique case, cardiac. The 650 skeletal striated muscles are attached to the bones to permit voluntary movements, which are consciously directed by the brain.

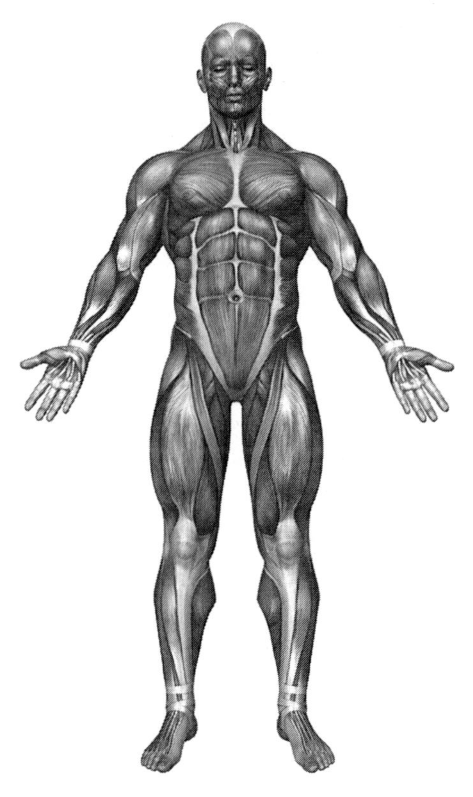

7

Even the ears and eyes have got muscles. The eye muscles are the most active ones, as they carry out about 100,000 movements per day. The strongest muscles in the body are the muscles called the masseters that we use for chewing our food. The smooth muscles also get directed by the brain but their motion is not voluntary, as in the case of digestion. Taking a step requires the use of 200 muscles. The heart is made up of cardiac muscle that beats automatically, 24 hours a day and never tires.

8

Fingers do not have muscles, but they have tendons—strings that join fingers to the arm muscles that make them move. The longest muscle in the body is the Sartorius which crosses and acts upon both the hip as well as the knee joints. The biggest muscle is the gluteus maximus, located in the buttock area. This muscle enables the movement of the hip as well as the thigh. Facial muscles help us form different facial expressions. During the process of cellular respiration, muscles use oxygen to produce energy from simple sugars like glucose. Exercising leads to an increase in our muscular and skeletal mass, improves muscle strength and flexibility.

9

Tongue is a hard worker in the body. It is considered the strongest muscle in the body and is made up of eight pairs of muscles but does not contain a bone. The tongue muscles help change the shape of the tongue by lengthening or shortening it, curling or uncurling it, and flattening and rounding its surface. The surface of the tongue can distinguish sweet, salty, sour and bitter flavours. There are about 10,000 taste buds on the tongue. It helps to eat and swallow food. It bends and contorts to help us form speech. It constantly releases saliva down the throat, even when we sleep. It contains lingual tonsils that filter out germs.

10

When we are fast asleep, that is when the brain is most active and busy gathering old memories, making new ones and connecting all those memories to your new ones. It also uses this time to detox itself and move recently gathered information to the long-term memory bank. Around 7,000 brain cells die as we reach the age of 35. The quality of food we consume over the lifetime affects the brain's functioning and structure. When we learn something new, we create a new connection, which results in the brain changing its structure.

11

Human brain is made up of tiny nerve cells, and is the most complex organ in the entire body that can store up to one quadrillion pieces of information. Though it represents only 2% of the total body weight, it keeps the body working and allows it to think, solve problems, learn and move in a well balanced way. Actions are controlled by the brain via a network of nerves that stretches throughout the body. Brain is a soft, spongy organ which is protected by a hard case known as the skull. Brain consists of three main parts: the cerebrum, cerebellum and brain stem. It uses 20% of the total oxygen and blood in the body, and it can only survive 4-6 minutes without oxygen.

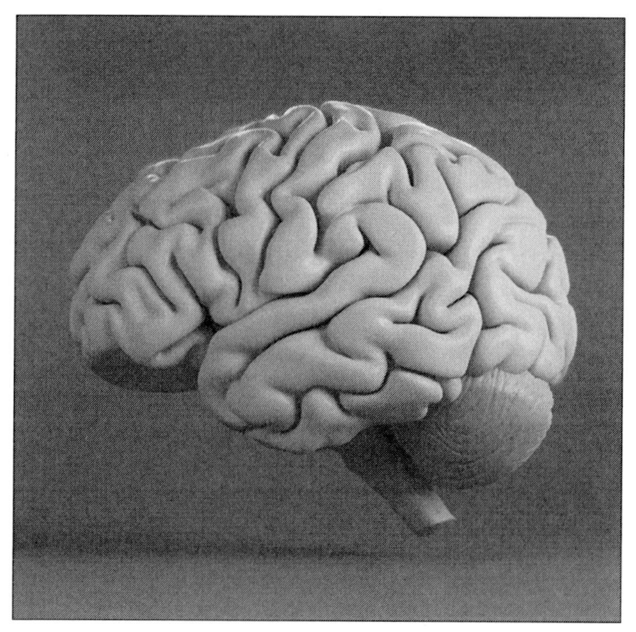

12

Our body is covered with a vast network of nerves that carry messages at a very high speed to inform the brain about the surroundings. Nerve impulses in the brain can travel as fast as 273 km per hour. If the central nervous system is damaged, it cannot repair itself on its own.

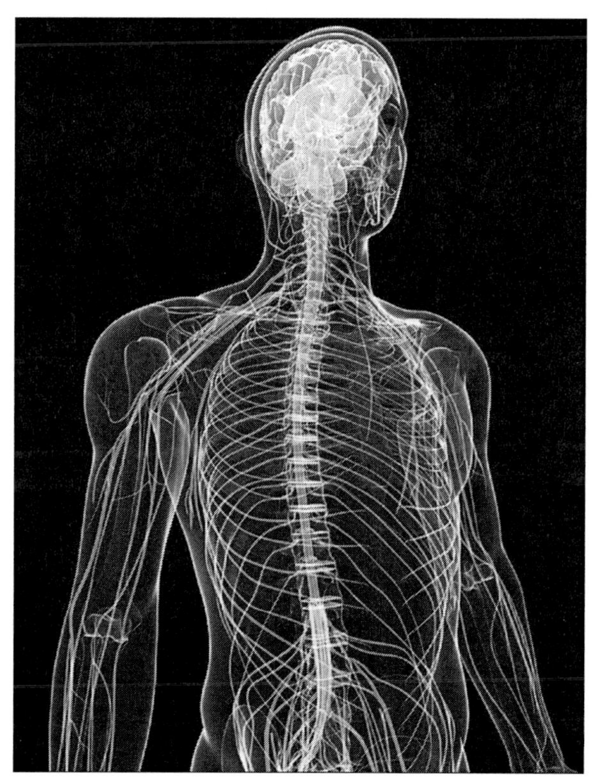

13

The spinal cord—a bundle of nerves and fibers, is attached to the brainstem and extends to the lower back. 33 vertebrae that form the spine, protect the spinal cord. Its main function is to transmit information between the brain and the spinal nerves. It consists of around 1,35,00,000 neurons that gather and transmit electrochemical signals.

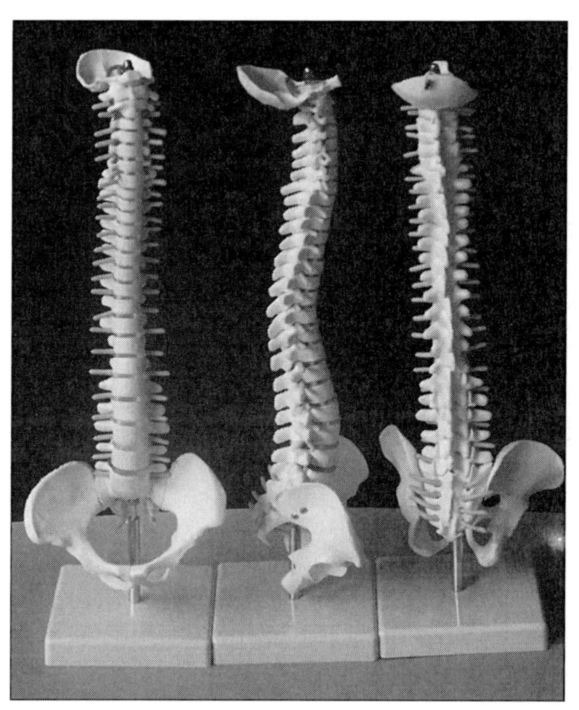

14

Brain does not have pain receptors. It can detect pain in any part of the body but in itself can not feel pain, even if a surgical procedure is performed on it. Pain during the headache arises from the pressure that is applied to the nerve tissues and not from the brain.

15

Nervous system needs Sodium and Potassium ions that perform the task of power generators inside cells, to function effectively. A good electrolyte balance is crucial for the blood, hydration and to maintain other important body functions.

16

All babies are born with blue eyes. The eye colour is revealed once the melanin (a pigment) is fully deposited or darkened by ultraviolet light. Genes determine the eye colour by dictating the amount of melanin produced in the iris. A low deposit of melanin in the irises makes them seem blue, while a medium amount makes them green or hazel and a lot makes them brown. All babies are colour blind at birth because the rods and cones, which allow for colour vision, have not yet been completely developed.

17

Eyes blink over six million times each year and each blink lasts only for 1/10th of a second. Eyelids spread oils and mucous secretions across the surface of the eyes every time we blink, to keep it moist and prevent dryness.

18

After an injury the blood forms blood clots to prevent the loss of blood. Platelets stick together to form a stopper that prevents bleeding. After the ruptured blood vessel heals, the solid clot dissolves in the blood. The body produces 200 billion platelets everyday, which are responsible for the clotting of blood and the formation of scabs.

19

The arteries, capillaries and veins in an adult would stretch out about 1,00,000 km, if they were to be laid out end-to-end.

20

There are about 5 billion red blood cells, half a million platelets and 7 thousand white blood cells in a drop of blood. The numbers of RBC are counted per cubic millimeter of blood, in a RBC count test. Normal red blood cell values for men are 4.6-6.0 million and for women are 4.2-5.0 million. Two million RBCs die every second and our bone marrow produces the same number each second. RBCs circle 75,000 times through the entire body in one lifespan.

21

Every day, our heart beats around 1,00,000 times, pumping around 7,570 litres of blood flowing through our body. A heartbeat is the sound that is produced by the closure of valves of the heart when the blood is pushed through its chamber.

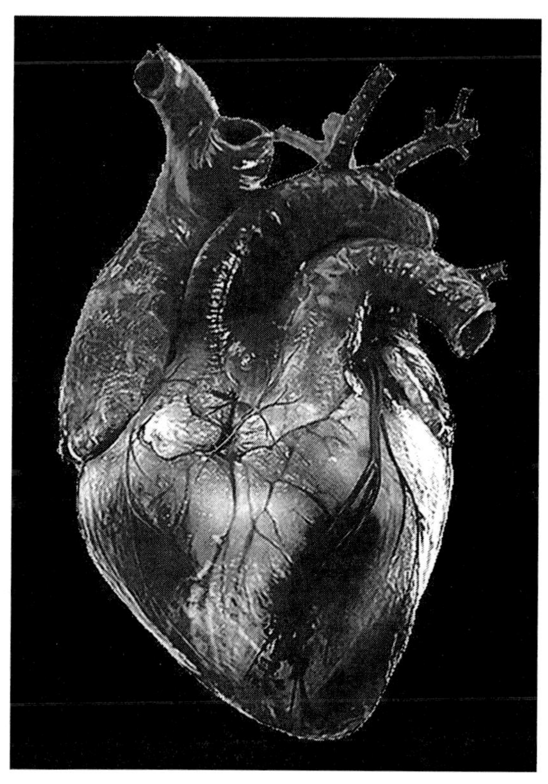

22

White cells in our body are not only produced in the blood but also in the spleen, liver and lymph glands. Most white cells are produced in our bone marrow from the same type of stem cells that produce RBCs. There are a total of around 30-40 billion white cells in our body that fight against infective and foreign organisms.

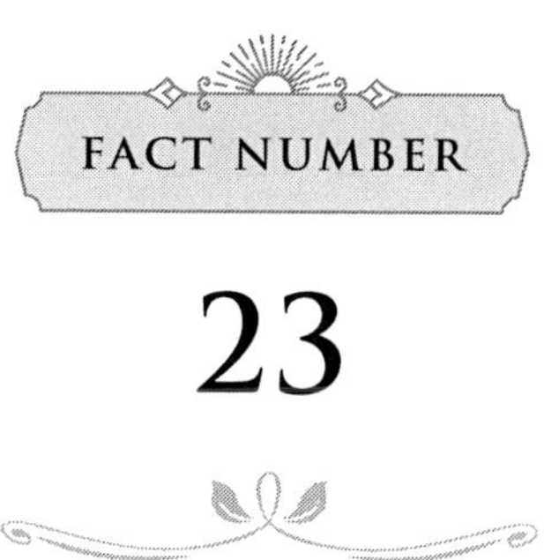

23

Capillaries running through almost every tissue of the body, are the smallest and the thinnest of the blood vessels in the body. They are about the one tenth of the diameter of a human hair. They help in the material exchange that occurs between the circulatory system and cells. The capillaries in the lungs would extend to 1,600 km if placed end to end.

24

Our lungs are not the same size. The right lung, which has three lobes is slightly larger than the left, which has only two lobes. If the lungs were stretched out flat, they would occupy the area half the size of a tennis court. They are the only organs that can float on water.

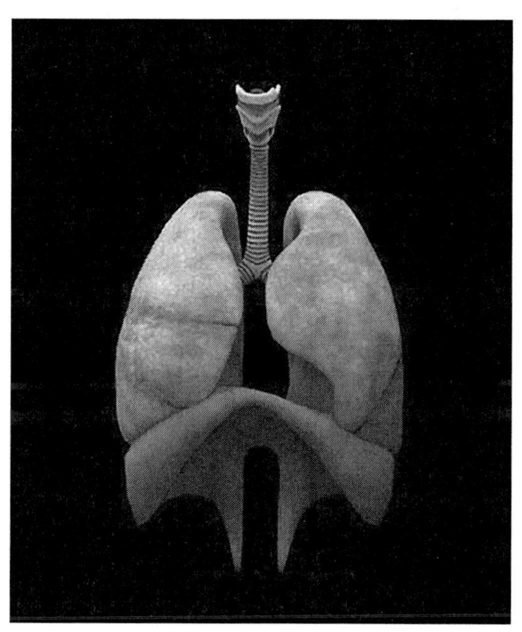

25

The adult body inhales and exhales about 6 litres of air each minute while resting. The normal respiration rate in adults is 12-16 breaths per minute and 45 breaths per minute during intense physical activity. We breathe almost 20,000 times a day.

26

The dome-shaped muscle at the bottom of the lungs called the diaphragm is the main muscle used in breathing. The intercostal muscles and the scalene muscles are used during inhalation. The abdominal muscles and internal intercostal muscles are used during exhalation, Hiccups are involuntary movements of the diaphragm.

27

Our body is made up of seven octillion atoms. Atoms are extremely small—a millionth of a millimetre across. Atoms are mostly just empty spaces and without these, we would fit into a box whose size is less than 1 cm.

28

Earlier studies showed that the human nose can discern 10,000 different types of odours. A recent observation suggested that the human nose can discern nearly a trillion smells and odours. The brain tells us whether a smell is pleasant or unpleasant. Over a time, we collect so many memories of different smells that we can even sense minor differences between various smells.

29

The cell along the inner lining of the stomach generates roughly 2 litres of hydrochloric acid every single day. It helps the stomach to kill illness-causing bacteria and break down the food we eat.

30

We produce more than a litre of saliva every day which combats tooth decay, breaks down food, helps us swallow, speak and gives us fresh breath. Saliva is made up of 99.5% water and 0.5% enzymes, mucus and other substances.

31

The process of digestion mostly takes place in the small intestine. The food that is swallowed makes its way from the throat to the oesophagus, which is 10 inches long and is pushed to the stomach in around seven seconds. The protein in the food is digested in the stomach. It mixes the food with digestive juices and sends the digested food to the small intestine in four to six hours. Nutrients are broken down into molecules to pass through the villi and into the bloodstream, and some are absorbed by the intestinal walls of the small intestine.

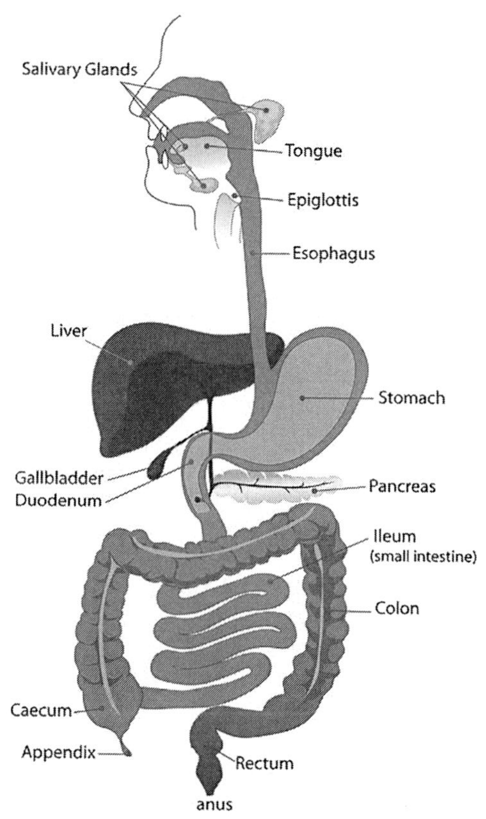

Salivary Glands
Tongue
Epiglottis
Esophagus
Liver
Stomach
Gallbladder
Duodenum
Pancreas
Ileum
(small intestine)
Colon
Caecum
Appendix
Rectum
anus

32

The adult stomach can expand and contract to accommodate food, and holds up to 1.5 litres of food when completely stuffed. The size of the stomach can change overtime due to overeating.

33

No digestion occurs in the large intestine, which is 1.5 m long. Around 1.5 litres of watery liquids enter the large intestine, where water reabsorption or recovery takes place.

34

We are not born with any bacteria in our digestive system. A significant amount is developed within the first month, most of which can be found in the large intestine. Bacteria fight off disease-carrying organisms, absorb nutrients that slip past the small intestine through fermentation and support the immune system.

35

Our body burns calories while digesting food. We require 5-15% energy to burn food and it varies depending on the type of food consumed. Protein accounts for 20-30% of the total energy expenditure of the body, while carbohydrates account for 5-10% and fats for 0-3%.

36

Our liver, being the largest and heaviest internal organ, performs 500 different functions. Its main function is to secrete bile into the small intestine during the digestion process. It also detoxifies blood and removes harmful substances from it. It stores vitamins, irons and simple sugar glucose. A healthy working liver processes 720 litres of blood every day.

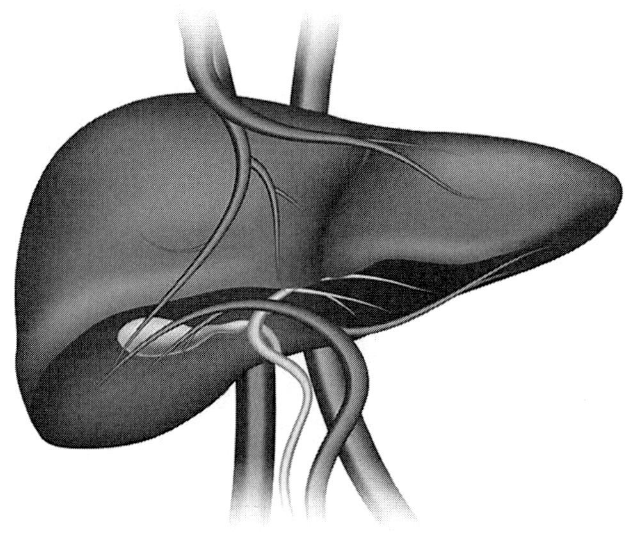

37

Our body burns one calorie for every kilogram of our weight depending on the number of hours we sleep. Our body uses those calories to perform certain important functions during the night, such as controlling the internal body temperature, pumping blood and repairing cells. It is the only organ that can regenerate lost tissues. A person requires a liver transplant if his liver loses that ability.

38

The human bladder can expand to hold about 400 ml of urine, which is produced by the kidneys. Urine can stay in the bladder for up to five hours before discharge. There are nerves in the bladder that send signals to the brain as to when the bladder needs to be emptied. Simultaneously, the brain signals the bladder muscles to tighten and the sphincter muscles to calm down, so the urine exits the bladder through the urethra normally.

39

The kidneys cleanses more than three million litres of water during a lifetime, which is more than sufficient to fill a small lake.

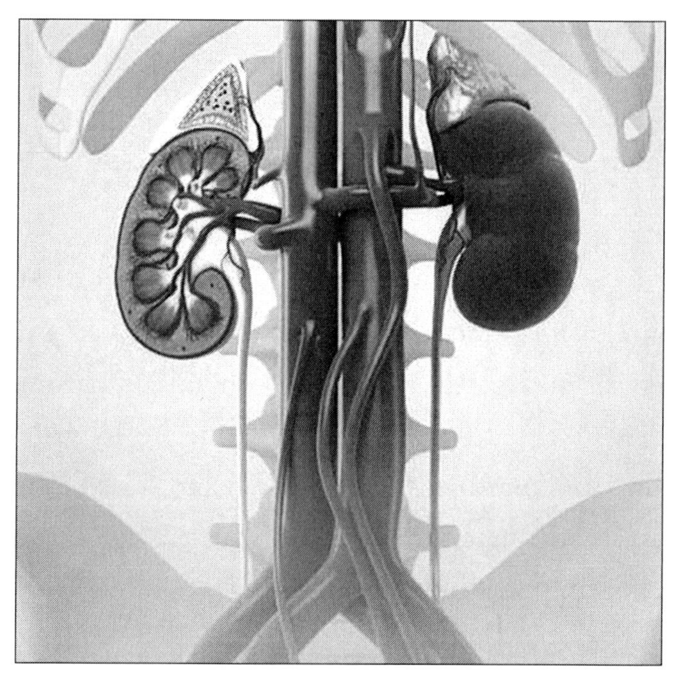

40

An average person passes 1.5 to 2 litres of urine in 24 hours. Urine is non-toxic and is a by-product of blood. It contains 95% water, 0.5% urea and 0.5% a mixture of minerals, salts and enzymes. It also contains urochrome—a pigmented blood product that gives urine its yellowish colour. Human urine is often diluted and added to plants due to its adequate urea content, which is a good source of nitrogen, potassium and phosphorus.

41

Kidneys are responsible for regulating the body's blood pressure in order to help sustain homeostasis. Each of the two kidneys is about 5.5 inches long and weighs about quarter of a kilogram. We can survive even with one kidney, as it can adapt to filter and perform just as two kidneys would do.

42

Kidneys produce a hormone called 'erythropoietin' that stimulates the production of RBCs in the body. 'Calcitriol' is another form of vitamin D, present in the human body, which the kidneys produce from precursor molecules. They also help to maintain mineral balance.

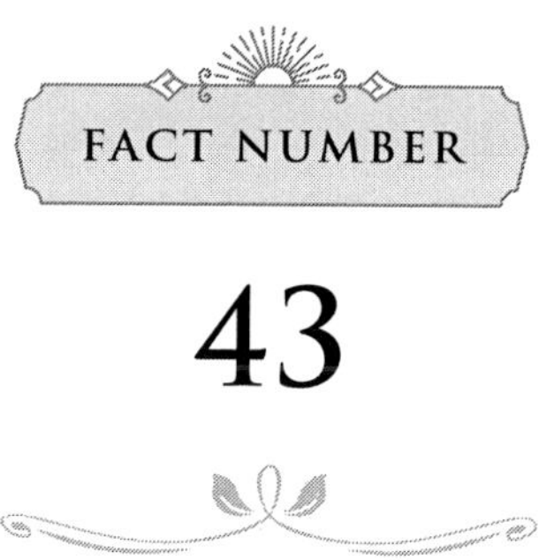

43

The parathyroid glands are embedded with one pair on either side in the surface of the thyroid gland. Normally the size of a grain of rice or as large as a pea, they release parathyroid hormone, which plays a role in maintaining calcium levels in the blood and bone metabolism.

44

The endocrine system secretes various hormones at higher than normal levels in response to stress, to help the body mobilise more energy and adapt to stress. Studies suggest that prolonged stressful vents can lead to endocrine disorders, including graves's disease, gonad dysfunction and obesity.

ENDOCRINE SYSTEM

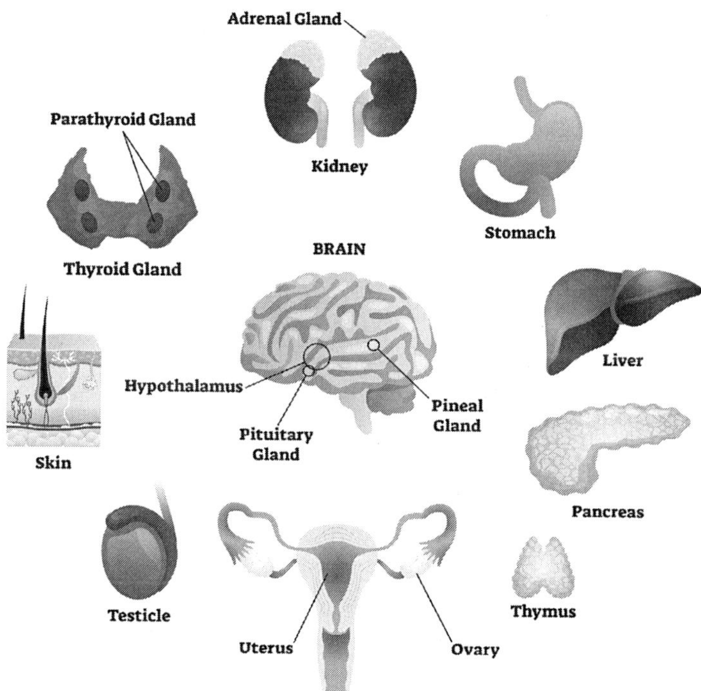

45

In 1902, the British researchers discovered that a chemical substance controlled activities involved in digestion. Since then more than 30 hormones produced by the human body have been identified. Hormones are chemical signals that manage various bodily functions, such as growth and development, metabolism, reproduction and response to stimuli.

46

There are around 2.6 million sweat glands in our body and out of these, 5,00,000 alone are in the feet and can produce more than a cup of sweat daily. Sweat glands can be found everywhere on the body, except the lips, nipples and genitals.

47

Only a few millimetres thick, the skin is the largest organ in the body, which weighs around 5 kg and has a surface area of almost 20 sq. ft. It forms the body's outer covering and a protective layer for the body from chemicals, diseases, ultraviolet light and physical damage. Hair and nails expand from the skin to strengthen it and protect it from environmental damage. Over 30,000 skin cells fall off every hour, which means we shed 4 kg of skin every year.

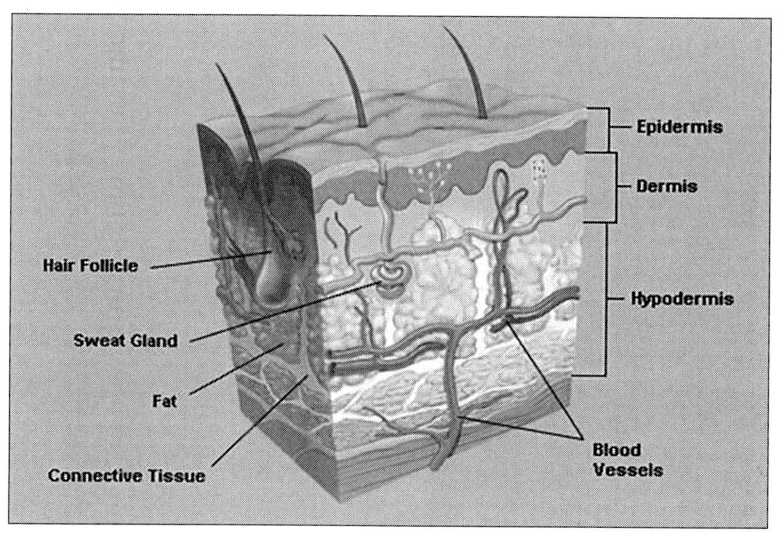

Epidermis
Dermis
Hypodermis
Hair Follicle
Sweat Gland
Fat
Connective Tissue
Blood
Vessels

48

90% of every hair strand consists of keratin and 5-10% water. Keratin is a fibrous protein, which gives strength and elasticity to the inner and outer structure of the hair. Keratin resists the harmful sun rays and cold winter breeze as well the heat of styling aids. Hair grows from the follicle that is underneath the skin. There are around 1,00,000 hair follicles on the scalp of a normal person. The hair strand that is above the skin has no biochemical activity. There is no pain and bleeding during a haircut because hair does not have any blood, nerve or muscle. The colour of the hair is defined by melanin and pheom-elanin, which are the main colour pigments inside the cortex. On average, we lose 50-100 strands of hair from the scalp per day.

49

The death of pigment cells in the hair follicles makes them turn grey. As people continue to grow older, fewer pigment cells will be present to produce the required amount of melanin. Genes are responsible for how early the hair turns grey.

50

Studies reveal that people who spend more time in the Sun are likely to be happier. The more sunlight the human body is exposed to, the more its brain produces serotonin; thereby leading the person to be happy and stay in a good mood.

51

Not all decisions are carefully controlled and thought out. Research states that most of the daily decisions are taken by the subconscious. Every second the brain is bombarded with 11 million individual pieces of data, which help make the necessary decision.

OTHER TITLES IN THIS SERIES

51 Must Know Facts About **Anne Frank**

51 Must Know Facts About **Blood**

51 Must Know Facts About **Brain**

51 Must Know Facts About **Diabetes**

51 Must Know Facts About **Heart**

51 Must Know Facts About **Human Body**

51 Must Know Facts About **Islam**

51 Must Know Facts About **Lungs**

51 Must Know Facts About **Pregnancy**

51 Must Know Facts About **Thomas Alva Edison**

- 12 Years A Slave by Solomon Northup, ISBN: 9789390492374

- 51 Must Know Facts About Albert Einstein by GP Editors, ISBN: 9789354991486

- 51 Must Know Facts About Brain by GP Editors, ISBN: 9789354994371

- A Theory of Human Motivation by Abraham H. Maslow, ISBN: 9789354993732

- Becoming a Writer by Dorothea Brande, ISBN: 9789389157093

- Believe in Yourself by Joseph Murphy, ISBN: 9789388118385

- Chanakya Neeti by Chanakya, ISBN: 9789389716276

- Children's Objective Quiz by Azeem Ahmad Khan, ISBN: 9788180320781

- Creative Mind and Success by Ernest Holmes, ISBN: 9789354994661

- Delighting in God by AW Tozer, ISBN: 9788194748632

- Feeling is the Secret by Neville Goddard, ISBN: 9789389157109

- Five Chimneys by Olga Lengyel, ISBN: 9789354991127

- Five Lessons by Neville Goddard, ISBN: 9789354991134

- Gravity by George Gamow, ISBN: 9789388118484

- Great Speeches of Abraham Lincoln, ISBN: 9789380914336

- How to Attract Money by Joseph Murphy, ISBN: 9789388118408

- How to Develop Self Confidence and... by Dale Carnegie, ISBN: 9789387669000

- How to Enjoy Your Life and Your Job by Dale Carnegie, ISBN: 9789387669017

- How to Own Your Own Mind by Napoleon Hill, ISBN: 9789354991189

- How to Stop Worrying and Start Living by Dale Carnegie, ISBN: 9789380914817

- How to Use the Power of Prayer by Joseph Murphy, ISBN: 9789354994395

- How to Win Friends and Influence People by Dale Carnegie, ISBN: 9788180320217

- If You Want to Write by Brenda Ueland, ISBN: 9789389716290

- Know Your Worth by NK Sondhi, ISBN: 9788180320231

- Life in Corona by NK Sondhi, ISBN: 9789354990571

PAPERBACK NON-FICTION

- Madhubala by Manju Gupta, ISBN: 9789380914961
- Mahatma Gandhi by Romain Rolland, ISBN: 9789354994456
- Meditation and Its Methods by Swami Vivekananda, ISBN: 9789389716320
- Meditations by Marcus Aurelius, ISBN: 9789388118736
- Mein Kampf by Adolf Hitler, ISBN: 9789380914855
- Memory by William Walker Atkinson, ISBN: 9789390492800
- My Inventions: An Autobiography by Nikola Tesla, ISBN: 9789388118132
- Quiz For All by Azeem Ahmad Khan, ISBN: 9788180320897
- State and Revolution by Vladimir Ilich Lenin, ISBN: 9789354990922
- Stolen Legacy by George J.M. James, ISBN: 9789354994494
- Success Through a Positi. Mental Attitude by Napoleon Hill, ISBN: 9789390492435
- Tao Te Ching by Lao Tzu, ISBN: 9788194764823
- The Alchemy of Happiness by Al-Ghazzali, ISBN: 9789387669505
- The Art of Living by Epictetus, ISBN: 9789354993817
- The Art of Public Speaking by Dale Carnegie, ISBN: 9788180320422
- The Autobiography of a Yogi by Paramahansa Yogananda, ISBN: 9789380914602
- The Complete Prophecies of Nostradamus by Nostradamus, ISBN: 9789354994234
- The Dhammapada by Gautama Buddha, ISBN: 9789390492817
- The Dynamic Laws of Prosperity by Catherine Ponder, ISBN: 9789388118156
- The Elements of Style by William Strunk, ISBN: 9789389157123
- The Federalist Papers by Alexander Hamilton, ISBN: 9789390492862
- The Interpretation of Dreams by Sigmund Freud, ISBN: 9789390492879
- The Knowledge of the Holy by AW Tozer, ISBN: 9789389157130
- The Kybalion: Philo. of Egypt & Greece by Three Initiates, ISBN: 9789354994579
- The Magic of Faith by Joseph Murphy, ISBN: 9789388118743

PAPERBACK NON-FICTION

- The Miracles of Your Mind by Joseph Murphy, ISBN: 9788180320743
- The Path of Prosperity by James Allen, ISBN: 9789387669512
- The Power of Concentration by Theron Q. Dumont, ISBN: 9789388118064
- The Power of the Spoken Word by Florence Scovel Shinn, ISBN: 9789390492893
- The Problem of Increasing Human Energy by Nikola Tesla, ISBN: 9789354990953
- The Problems of Philosophy by Bertrand Russell, ISBN: 9789354994296
- The Quick and Easy Way to Effec. Speaking by Dale Carnegie, ISBN: 9789387669031
- The Science of Being Great by Wallace D. Wattles, ISBN: 9789354993886
- The Science of Getting Rich by Wallace D. Wattles, ISBN: 9788180320972
- The Science of Mind by Ernest Holmes, ISBN: 9789354993909
- The Secret of Imagining by Neville Goddard, ISBN: 9789354991271
- The Secret Teachings of All Ages by Manly P. Hall, ISBN: 9789390492046
- The Seven Laws of Teaching by John Milton Gregory, ISBN: 9789387669413
- The Story of My Life by Helen Keller, ISBN: 9789380914541
- The Success System that Never Fails by W.C. Stone, ISBN: 9789390492114
- The Ultimate Guide To Success by Julia Seton, ISBN: 9789390492350
- The Wit and Wisdom of Gandhi by Mahatma Gandhi, ISBN: 9789380914039
- The Yoga Sutras of Patanjali by Patanjali, ISBN: 9789389716351
- Think and Grow Rich by Napoleon Hill, ISBN: 9788180320255
- Thought Vibration by William Walker Atkinson, ISBN: 9789389157154
- Thoughts are Things by Prentice Mulford, ISBN: 9789354994326
- Up From Slavery by Booker T. Washington, ISBN: 9789380914565
- Value, Price, and Profit by Karl Marx, ISBN: 9789354993978
- Wake Up and Live by Dorothea Brande, ISBN: 9789387669574
- Who were the Shudras by Dr. B.R. Ambedkar, ISBN: 9789354991028

Develop your reading habit | **Gift books to your friends**